The World of

Barbie Dolls

An Illustrated Value Guide

Paris & Susan Manos

COLLECTOR BOOKS

A Division of Schroeder Publishing Co., Inc.

The current values in this book should be used only as a guide. They are not intended to set prices, which vary from one section of the country to another. Auction prices as well as dealer prices vary greatly and are affected by condition as well as demand. Neither the Author nor the Publisher assumes responsibility for any losses that might be incurred as a result of consulting this guide.

The prices shown in this guide are derived by the authors, wholly independent of Mattel and Mattel has no connection therewith.

This book makes reference to BARBIE® and other identities for various dolls produced by Mattel, Inc. which are trademarks of Mattel.

Dedication

This book is dedicated to Mattel, for giving us so much joy through a doll named BARBIE®.

We would like to say thank you to Carol Manos, Margaret Haley, Jane Horvath, Carline Irish, Bernice Lelito, and Mariann Ocker.

Foreword

It is magic – this world of Barbie doll collecting. How else can we be transported back into the joys of yesterday, the realities of today, and the anticipation of tomorrow? This book is ambitious in scope as it brings to us a visual image of many of the early Barbie dolls, costumes, and accessories set in their proper sequence. The color photography captures the glamour and magnificence of these early gowns.

We are indeed grateful to the Manos family for bringing us another informative and readable book on one of our favorite subjects.

Look through these pages and share with us the thrill of collecting.

Margaret T. Haley
The Barbie Doll Collector's Club
Great Lakes Chapter

Introduction

The World of Barbie Dolls, truly the title of this book, tells it all — and what a wonderful world it is.

We have structured this book in full color, to share with you some of the delights and intrigue of Barbie doll collecting as well as an understanding of value.

Pricing Guide

Pricing in this book is based on mint-in-box (M.I.B.) dolls. This means never removed from the original package. At least 20% of the M.I.B. value is taken off a doll once it has been removed from the original packaging. A mint doll in its original (manufactured) garb, minus box, is 50% less than the M.I.B. value. Pricing beyond this scale is left to the discretion of the individual.

Table of Contents

Barbie Dolls And Female Friends

1959 #1 Barbie doll with holes lined with copper tubing under feet. Blonde, $1,200.00 M.I.B.; brunette, $1,500.00 M.I.B. The brunette is harder to find (only one out of every three #1 Barbie dolls was brunette.)

Close-up of blonde and brunette #1 Barbie dolls. Note peaked eyebrows, no iris color, and slight blue liner over eye lashes.

1959 #2 Barbie doll. Blonde, $1,000.00 M.I.B.; brunette, $1,100.00 M.I.B. (harder to find). This doll looks like the #1 Barbie doll except it does not have holes in the feet. #2 Barbie dolls are much harder to find, but they are not as popular as the #1 Barbie doll.

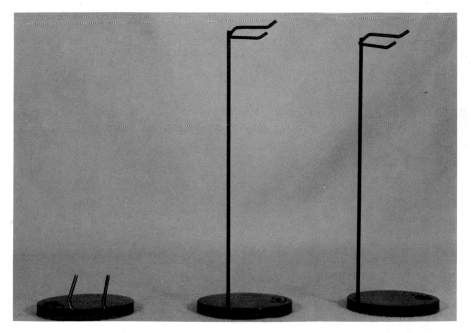

#1 stand, $100.00 and up; #2 stand, $75.00 and up; #3 stand, $60.00 and up.

1960 #3 unusual blonde Barbie doll. Note the holes at the soles of her feet like a #1 doll. This is referred to as a transitional doll. #3 blonde Barbie doll with brown eye liner, $500.00 M.I.B.

1960 #3 brunette pony tail Barbie doll had soft, curly bangs. This doll is harder to find than the blonde, $400.00 M.I.B.; #3 blonde pony tail Barbie doll also has soft curly bangs. This doll has blue eye liner, which is harder to find than one with brown, $300.00 M.I.B.

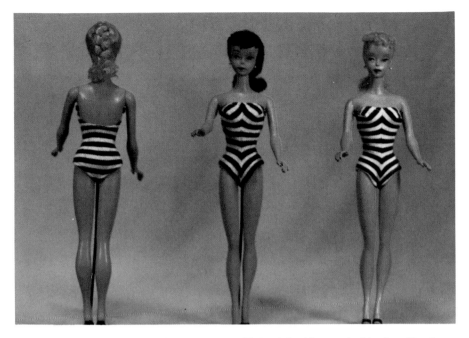

1960 #4 Barbie doll. First four issues (#1, #2, #3 & #4) had heavy vinyl bodies. The first three issues faded in color but the #4 retained its flesh-tone color. Note the different hairdo. #4 blonde, $250.00 M.I.B.; #4 brunette, $270.00 M.I.B.

1961 #5, the first hollow-bodied Barbie doll. They came with pony tails and coarse, curly bangs. They came with blonde, brunette, or red hair. $125.00 M.I.B.

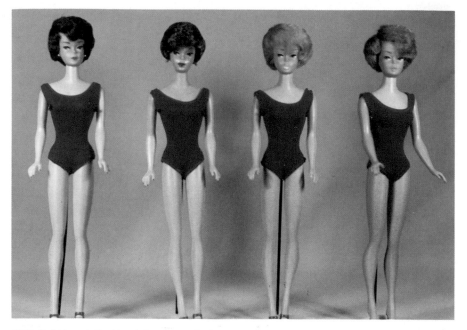

1962 Bubble-cut Barbie dolls. Came in brunette, brown, blonde, and redhead. $100.00 M.I.B.

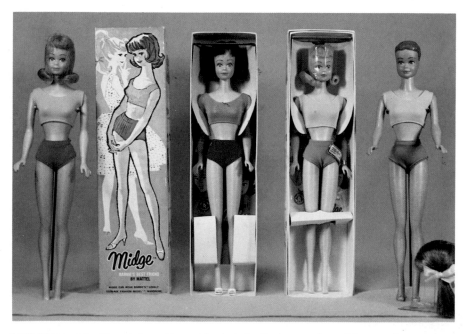

1963 Midge doll with red, brunette, or blonde hair. Each came in a different colored suit. •
$125.00 M.I.B. The painted-hair Midge doll is a put-together doll with a Midge Wig Wardrobe head.

Close-up of unusual 1963 Midge doll with teeth and side-glance eyes. $200.00 M.I.B.

Close-up of a very unusual 1963 freckleless Midge doll. This doll is mint in box and has a beautiful skin coloring. Very hard to find, $450.00 M.I.B.

1963 "Fashion Queen" Barbie doll. This doll came with three interchangeable wigs and wig stand. $200.00 M.I.B.

1964 Swirl pony tail Barbie dolls, redhead, brunette, and blonde. $175.00 M.I.B.

1965 first bendable leg Barbie doll with new short hairstyle. This hairstyle is referred to as the American Girl or Dutch boy style. $200.00 M.I.B.

Close-up of 1965 very hard to find, side-part bendable leg Barbie doll. $900.00 M.I.B.

1964 "Miss Barbie" doll, often referred to as "Sleep-Eyed Barbie." This doll came with three interchangeable wigs, a wig stand, and lawn swing with accessories. $500.00 M.I.B. Doll in mint condition with suit, cap and wig wardrobe, $200.00. Note extra head. These are unpainted and were never put on bodies. They were never put on the market.

1965 bendable leg Midge doll. This was the last issue of the Midge dolls. Hard to find, $250.00 M.I.B.

1965 "Color Magic" Barbie doll. These dolls had bendable legs and changeable hair coloring. $400.00 M.I.B. Color Magic Barbie dolls came with two hair colors. Golden Blonde changed to Scarlet Flame and back again, and Midnight Black changed to Ruby Red. Swimsuit colors could also change. Green diamonds changed to purple, yellow diamonds changed to red, and back again.

1966 Twist 'N Turn Barbie doll, $100.00 M.I.B.; 1967 Twist 'N Turn Barbie doll, $100.00 M.I.B.; 1968 Twist 'N Turn Barbie doll $100.00 M.I.B.; 1969 Twist 'N Trun Barbie doll, $100.00 M.I.B.; 1971 Twist 'N Turn Barbie doll, $75.00 M.I.B.

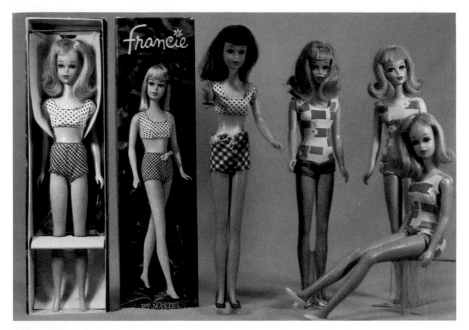

1966 Francie doll. Straight leg Francie doll, $100.00 M.I.B.; bendable leg Francie doll, $90.00 M.I.B.

1967 Black Francie doll. Second issue with dark eyes and dark brown hair, $400.00 M.I.B.; 1967 Black Francie doll, first issue with light brown eyes and red oxidized hair, $450.00 M.I.B.; 1967 Twist 'N Turn Francie doll, $60.00 M.I.B.

1967 blonde and brunette Casey dolls, M.I.B. $125.00 each.

1967 Twiggy doll, a personality doll. Looks like the Casey doll only hair is shorter and she wears heavier eye make-up. $125.00 M.I.B.

1970 Standard Barbie doll, $175.00 M.I.B.; 1967 Standard Barbie, $90.00 M.I.B.

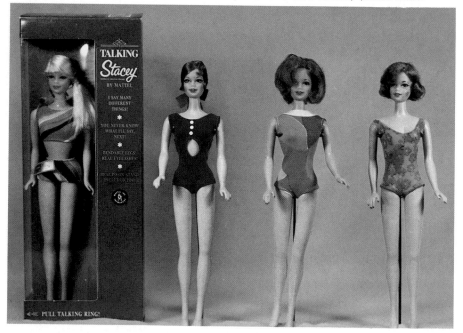

1968 Talking Stacey doll, $90.00 M.I.B.; 1968 Twist 'N Turn Stacey doll, $90.00 M.I.B.; 1969 Twist 'N Turn Stacey doll, $85.00 M.I.B.; 1969 very hard to find Twist 'n Turn Stacey doll, $110.00 M.I.B. only.

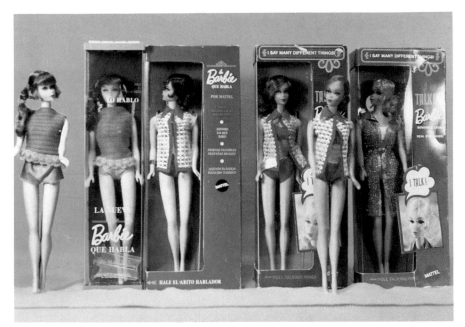

1968 Talking Barbie doll, $110.00 M.I.B.; 1968 & 1969 Spanish Talking Barbie doll, 175.00 M.I.B. only; 1969 Talking Barbie doll, $110.00 M.I.B.; 1971 Talking Barbie doll, $110.00 M.I.B.

1969 New 'N Groovy Talking P.J. doll, $90.00 M.I.B.; 1969 Twist 'N Turn P.J. doll, $80.00 M.I.B.

1969 Talking Truly Scrumptious doll, $325.00 M.I.B.; 1969 Standard Truly Scrumptious doll, $375.00 M.I.B.

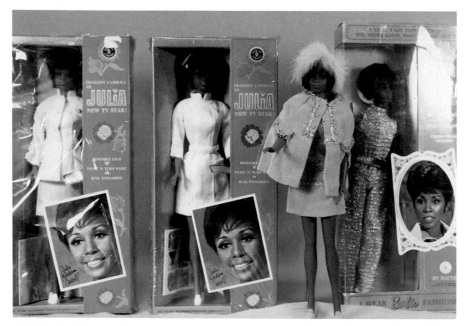

1969 Twist 'N Turn Julia doll in hard to find two-piece nurse's uniform, $80.00 M.I.B.; 1970 Twist 'N Turn Julia doll, $80.00 M.I.B.; 1969 Talking Julia doll, $70.00 M.I.B.

1971 Twist 'N Turn Francie doll, often referred to as "No Bangs Francie," hard to find. Blonde and brunette, $425.00 M.I.B.; 1969 Twist 'N Turn Francie doll, $85.00 M.I.B.; 1970 Twist 'N Turn Francie doll, $85.00 M.I.B.

1970 Francie doll "With Growin' Pretty Hair," $95.00 M.I.B.; 1970 Francie doll "Hair Happenin's," $110.00 M.I.B.

1969 New Talking Christie doll, $70.00 M.I.B.; 1970 Talking Christie doll, $70.00 M.I.B.; 1969 Twist Christie doll, $70.00 M.I.B.; 1971 Live Action Christie doll, $90.00 M.I.B.

1970 Walking Jamie doll, $150.00 M.I.B.; 1970 Walking Jamie doll with dog, part of a Sears gift set (see gift set chapter).

1971 Dramatic New Living Barble doll, $85.00 M.I.B.; 1969 Living Barbie doll, $95.00 M.I.B.; Living Barbie doll from Japan, Sears gift set (see gift set chapter).

1971 "Live Action Barbie On Stage," $85.00 M.I.B.; 1971 Live Action Barbie doll, $75.00 M.I.B.

1971 "Live Action P.J. On Stage," $85.00 M.I.B.; Live Action P.J. doll, $75.00 M.I.B.

1971 Barbie doll "With Growin' Pretty Hair," $200.00 M.I.B.; 1971 Barbie "Hair Happenin's," Sears limited edition, very hard to find, $425.00 M.I.B.; 1972 Barbie "With Growin' Pretty Hair." This doll is harder to find than the 1971 issue. $225.00 M.I.B.

1972 Walk Lively Barbie and Steffie dolls, M.I.B., $85.00 each.

1972 "Busy Barbie with Holdin' Hands," $100.00 M.I.B.; 1972 "Talking Busy Barbie with Holdin' Hands," $150.00 M.I.B.

1971 Malibu Barbie doll and 1972 Malibu P.J. doll. M.I.B., $30.00 each.

1972 Walk Lively "Miss American" doll. Promotional from the Kellog Co., $60.00 M.I.B.;
Blonde Quick Curl "Miss America" doll from Canada, $60.00 M.I.B.; Blonde Quick Curl
"Miss America" doll offered at most stores, $45.00 M.I.B.; Brunette Quick Curl "Miss
America" doll with longer hair and twist waist. This doll is harder to find, $210.00 M.I.B.

1972 "Busy Steffie with Holdin' Hands," $100.00 M.I.B.; 1972 "Busy Talking Steffie with Holdin' Hands," $150.00 M.I.B.

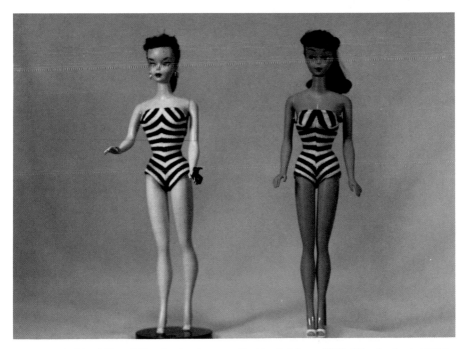

1959 #1 Barbie doll and Ward's Anniversary Barbie doll from 1972. Ward's Anniversary doll, $325.00 M.I.B.

Rare Francie doll from Germany, very hard to find (not priced). 1971 & 1972 Malibu Francie doll, $30.00 M.I.B.

1972 "Busy Francie with Holdin' Hands," $150.00 M.I.B.; 1973 Quick Curl Francie doll, $45.00 M.I.B.

1973 Quick Curl Barbie doll with extra outfit. This was a store promotion issue, $125.00 mint on card; 1973 Quick Curl Barbie doll. Sold in most stores. $45.00 M.I.B.

1973 Quick Curl Kelley doll. Two different versions of packaging. $80.00 M.I.B.; 1973 Quick Curl Cara doll from Canada, $50.00 M.I.B.

Collection of Malibu dolls from 1971-1974. M.I.B. $30.00 each.

Collection of 1975 "Gold Medal" Barbie dolls. Skater, $45.00 M.I.B.; Winter Sports, $35.00 M.I.B.; Olympic Sports, $35.00 M.I.B.; Skier, $45.00 M.I.B.

1974 Sun Valley Barbie doll, $55.00 M.I.B.

1974 "Sweet Sixteen" Barbie doll, $40.00 M.I.B.; 1974 "Sweet Sixteen" Barbie doll with promotional outfit on card, $55.00 M.I.B.

Two different versions of packaging of 1974 "Yellowstone Kelley." Hard to find, $125.00
M.I.B. Two different versions of packaging of 1974 Newport Barbie doll, $70.00 M.I.B.

1975 Free Moving P.J. doll, Cara doll, and Barbie doll. M.I.B. $50.00 each.

1976 Deluxe Quick Curl P.J. doll, Barbie doll, and Cara doll. M.I.B. $40.00 each.

1976 "Beautiful Bride Barbie," first issue, a department store special, $150.00 M.I.B.;
1976 "Beautiful Bride Barbie," sold in most stores, $50.00 M.I.B.

1976 Ballerina Barbie doll. First issue with hair pulled to back of head, $40.00 M.I.B.; 1978 Ballerina Barbie doll. Second issue with heavier eye make-up and side curl added, $30.00 M.I.B.; 1976 Ballerina Cara doll, $40.00 M.I.B.

1976 "Ballerina Barbie On Tour." This was a department store special (not shown). $50.00 M.I.B.; 1978 re-issue "Ballerina Barbie On Tour." Three costume variations, sold in selected stores, $50.00 M.I.B.

Collection of "Baggie" dolls. Ken doll, $30.00 mint in package; Malibu Skipper doll, mint in package, $20.00; Malibu Barbie doll and P.J. doll, mint in package, $20.00 each; Francie doll and Casey doll, mint in package, $20.00 each; Pose 'n Play Skipper doll, mint in package, $25.00.

1976 Fold-out booklet, Super Star Barbie doll. First issue, promo with extra hair comb, $80.00 M.I.B.; Second issue, promo with extra necklace, $60.00 M.I.B.; Super Star Christie doll, $40.00 M.I.B.; Super Star Gift Sets. These were sold in selected stores only, $70.00 M.I.B.

Barbie Doll's Male Friends

1961 First issue flocked hair Ken doll came with bathing trunks, sandals, and towel. $125.00 M.IB.; 1961 Second issue Ken doll with flocked hair, $80.00 M.I.B.; 1962 Painted hair Ken doll, $75.00 M.I.B.; 1963 Allen Doll, $70.00 M.I.B.

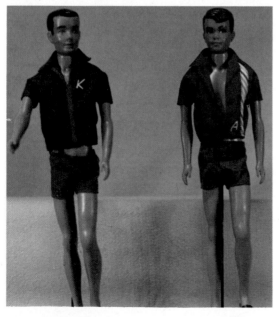

1964 Bendable leg Ken doll and Bendable leg Allen doll. These dolls are harder to find, $200.00 M.I.B.

1969 Ken returns with a new look. Talking Ken doll, $75.00 M.I.B.; 1969 Spanish Talking Ken doll, M.I.B. only, $75.00; 1969 Talking Brad doll, $75.00 M.I.B.

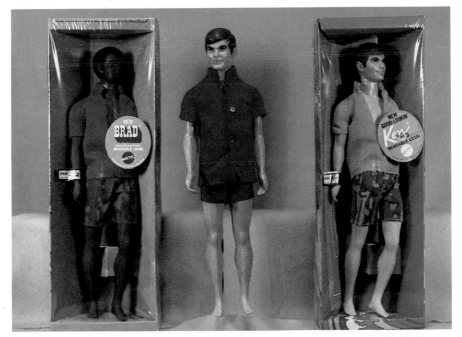

1971 Bendable leg Brad doll, $70.00 M.I.B.; 1969 Bendable leg Ken doll, $75.00 M.I.B.; 1970 Bendable leg Ken doll, $70.00 M.I.B.

1971 Live Action Ken doll, $70.00 M.I.B.; 1971 "Live Action Ken On Stage," $80.00
M.I.B.; 1972 Walk Lively Ken doll, $80.00 M.I.B.

1972 Busy Ken doll, $100.00 M.I.B.; 1972 Talking Busy Ken doll, $125.00 M.I.B.

1973 Mod Hair Ken doll, $45.00 M.I.B.; 1976 Now Look Ken doll, two versions, $45.00 M.I.B.

1971-1974 Malibu Ken dolls, M.I.B. $30.00 each.

1974 Sun Valley Ken doll, $70.00 M.I.B.; 1975 "Gold Medal" Ken Skier doll, $60.00 M.I.B.

1975 Free Moving Ken doll, $40.00 M.I.B.; 1975 Free Moving Curtis doll. This doll was only out for one year. Hard to find, $55.00 M.I.B.

1978 "Super Star Barbie and Ken" set. This was a department store special. $110.00 M.I.B.; 1976 First issue Super Star Ken doll with extra ring for the little girl to play with, $45.00 M.I.B.

3 different Canadian Ken dolls. 1979 Sports Star Ken doll, $40.00 M.I.B.; 1980 Golden Night Ken doll, $35.00 M.I.B.; 1981 Jogging Ken doll, $30.00 M.I.B.

The Younger Set

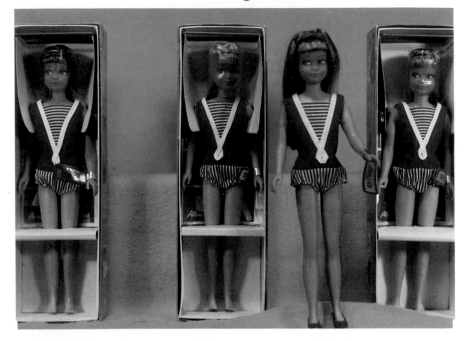

1964 Skipper doll with three different hair colorings, $80.00 M.I.B.

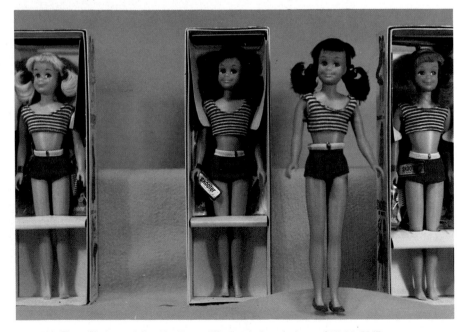

1964 First Skooter doll with three different hair colorings, $95.00 M.IB.

1965 Ricky doll. This doll was produced only for a short time and it is not easy to find mint in box. $85.00 M.I.B.

1965 First Bendable leg Skipper doll, $90.00 M.I.B.; 1966 Bendable leg Skooter doll was discontinued shortly after this issue, $100.00 M.I.B.

1966 Tutti doll, came with blonde or brunette hair, $60.00 M.I.B.; 1966 Todd doll, hard to find, $65.00 M.I.B.; 1967 Chris doll, hard to find, $60.00 M.I.B.; 1967 Tutti doll, $60.00 M.I.B.

1966 "Me and My Dog" Tutti doll play set, $200.00 M.I.B.; 1966 "Sundae Treat" Tutti and Todd dolls play set, $250.00 M.I.B.

1966 "Walking My Dolly" Tutti doll play set, $100.00 M.I.B. This set was re-issued in Europe in 1975 (not shown.) $60.00 M.I.B.; 1966 "Melody in Pink" Tutti doll play set, $185.00 M.I.B. The dress came in two different color variations.

1967 "Cookin' Goodies" Tutti doll play set, $175.00 M.I.B.; 1966 "Night Night Sleep Tight" Tutti doll play set, $90.00 M.I.B. This set was re-issued in Europe in 1975 (not shown.) $60.00 M.I.B.

1975 "Swing-a-ling" Tutti doll play set. This is a re-issued set from Europe. $75.00 M.I.B.; 1967 "Swing-a-ling" Tutti doll play set. This is the original and is the hardest of all play sets to find, $250.00 M.I.B.

1967 re-issued Bendable leg Skipper doll, rare when M.I.B. only, $95.00; 1968 Twist 'N Turn Skipper doll, $65.00 M.I.B.; 1969 New Twist 'N Turn Skipper doll, $65.00 M.I.B.; 1970 Twist Skipper doll, $65.00 M.I.B.

1970 New Living Skipper doll, $65.00 M.I.B.; 1971 Fluff doll, $70.00 M.I.B.; 1972 Tiff doll, hard to find, $225.00 M.I.B.

1968 Buffy and Mrs. Beasley dolls, $90.00 M.I.B.; 1970 Pretty Pairs — "Angie 'N Tangie," Lori 'N Rori," "Nan 'N Fran," M.I.B. $175.00 each.

1973 Pose 'N Play Skipper doll (baggie), mint in package, $15.00; 1973 Quick Curl Skipper doll, $30.00 M.I.B.; 1971 Malibu Skipper doll, $15.00 M.I.B.

1975 "Growing Up" Skipper doll, $45.00 M.IB.; 1976 "Growing Up" Ginger doll, $45.00 M.I.B.

1967 Tutti doll, $40.00 M.I.B.; 1967 Todd doll, $40.00 M.I.B.; 1967 Chris doll, $40.00 M.I.B.; European re-issued Tutti doll, $25.00 M.I.B.; European re-issued Todd doll, $25.00 M.I.B.

European re-issued Chris doll, $45.00 M.I.B.; European re-issued Carla doll, $45.00 M.I.B.

Hard To Find Outfits

In this chapter we have included outfits that are not hard to find singly, but are difficult to collect as a set. Go-together outfits or matched outfits for the Barbie doll and Skipper doll, Little Theatre, and Travel groups fall into this category. Although some outfits are not unusual, a variation might be.

You will see photographed here a few outfits that were never pictured in booklets. Those that were are dated according to the year they first appeared in a booklet. **Prices given are for outfit only.**

Three of the most wanted outfits among Barbie doll collectors. "Easter Parade" outfit #971 (#1 1958 booklet), $275.00 M.I.B.; "Gay Parisienne" outfit #968 (#1 1958 booklet), $275.00 M.IB.; "Roman Holiday" outfit #964 (#1 1958 booklet), $275.00 M.I.B.

"Solo In The Spotlight" outfit #962 (#2 1958 booklet), $55.00 M.I.B.; "Enchanted Evening" outfit #983 (#2 1958 booklet), $65.00 M.I.B.

"Plantation Belle" outfit #966 (#2 1958 booklet), $50.00 M.I.B.; "Picnic Set" outfit #967 (#2 1958 booklet), $60.00 M.I.B.; "Busy Gal" outfit #981 (#2 1958 booklet), $70.00 M.I.B.; "Commuter Set" outfit #916 (#2 1958 booklet), $90.00 M.I.B.

Skipper doll in "Flower Girl" outfit #1904 (1962 booklet), $30.00 M.I.B.; Barbie doll in "Barbie's Dream" outfit #947 (1962 booklet), $50.00 M.I.B.; Midge doll in "Orange Blossom" outfit #987 (1962 booklet), $30.00 M.I.B.

51

Ken doll in "Tuxedo" outfit #787 (1961 booklet), $75.00 M.I.B.; Barbie doll in "Wedding Day Set" outfit #972 (1961 booklet), $80.00 M.I.B.

Barbie doll in "Sophisticated Lady" outfit #993 (1963 booklet), $75.00 M.I.B.; Barbie doll in "Midnight Blue" outfit #1617 (1964 booklet) $125.00 M.I.B.

Barbie doll in "Reception Line" outfit #1654 (1965 booklet), $95.00 M.I.B.; Barbie doll in "Garden Wedding" outfit #1658 (1965 booklet), $60.00 M.I.B.; Allan doll in "Best Man" outfit #1425 (1965 booklet), $95.00 M.I.B.

Tutti doll in "Flower Girl" outfit #3615 (1966 booklet), $45.00 M.I.B.; Skipper doll in "Junior Bridesmaid" outfit #1934 (1965 booklet), $65.00 M.I.B.; Todd doll in "Ring Bearer" outfit from Europe (1976), $20.00 M.I.B.

Ken doll in "Here Comes The Groom" outfit #1426 (1965 booklet), $150.00 M.I.B.; Barbie doll in "Here Comes The Bride" outfit #1665 (1965 booklet), $150.00 M.I.B.

Barbie doll in "Holiday Dance" outfit #1639 (1964 booklet), $65.00 M.I.B.; Barbie doll in "Campus Sweetheart" outfit #1616, very hard to find, $90.00 M.I.B.

Barbie doll in "Pink Formal" outfit (Sears Exclusive), $125.00 M.I.B. This outfit is known by two names – "Magnificence" #1649 (1964 booklet) and "Fabulous Fashion" #1676 (1965 booklet), $100.00 M.I.B.

Barbie doll in "Fraternity Dance" outfit #1638 (1964 booklet), $75.00 M.I.B.; Barbie doll in "Junior Prom" outfit #1614 (1964 booklet), $75.00 M.I.B.

Barbie doll in "Golden Glory" outfit #1645 (1965 booklet), $70.00 M.I.B.; Barbie doll in "Benefit Performance" outfit #1667 (1965 booklet), very hard to find, $100.00 M.I.B.; Barbie doll in "Debutante Ball" outfit #1666 (1965 booklet), very hard to find, $100.00 M.I.B.

Barbie doll in "Evening Gala" outfit #1660 (1965 booklet), $65.00 M.I.B.; Barbie doll in "Patio Party" outfit #1692 (1966 booklet), $60.00 M.I.B.

Julia doll in "Evening Enchantment" outfit #1695 (1966 booklet), very hard to find. $90.00 M.I.B.; Brad doll in "Groovy Formal" outfit #1431 (1969 booklet), $35.00 M.I.B.

"Barbie Fashion Pak": "Ruffles 'N Lace" (1963 booklet), mint in package, $15.00; Skipper doll in "Under-Pretties" outfit #1900 (1963 booklet), $15.00 M.I.B.; Barbie doll in "Nighty-Negligee" outfit #965 (#1 1958 booklet), $35.00 M.I.B.; Skipper doll in "Dreamtime" outfit #1909 (1963 booklet), $25.00 M.I.B.

Barbie doll in "Silken Flame" outfit #977 (1962 booklet), $25.00 M.I.B.; Skipper doll in "Silk 'N Fancy" outfit #1902 (1963 booklet), $20.00 M.I.B.; Barbie doll in "Red Flare" outfit #939 (1962 booklet), $25.00 M.I.B.; Skipper doll in "Dress Coat" outfit #1906 (1963 booklet), $20.00 M.I.B.

Barbie doll in "Ballerina" outfit #989 (1961 booklet), $25.00 M.I.B.; Skipper doll in "Ballet Class" outfit #1905 (1963 booklet), $20.00 M.I.B.; Barbie doll in "Icebreaker" outfit #942 (1962 booklet), $30.00 M.I.B.; Skipper doll in "Skating Fun" outfit #1908 (1963 booklet), $25.00 M.I.B.

Midge doll in "Orange Blossom" outfit #987 (1961 booklet), $30.00 M.I.B.; Skipper doll in "Flower Girl" outfit #1904 (1963 booklet), $30.00 M.I.B.; Barbie doll in "Sheath Sensation" outfit #986 (1961 booklet), $20.00 M.I.B.; Skipper doll in "Red Sensation" outfit #1901 (1963 booklet), $20.00 M.I.B.

Barbie doll in "Dancing Doll" outfit #1626 (1964 booklet), $45.00 M.I.B.; Skipper doll in "Me 'N My Doll" outfit #1913 (1964 booklet), $65.00 M.I.B.

Barbie doll in "Fun At The Fair" outfit #1624 (1964 booklet), $50.00 M.I.B.; Skipper doll in "Day At The Fair" outfit #1911 (1964 booklet), $70.00 M.I.B.

Barbie doll in "Riding In The Park" outfit #1668 (1965 booklet), $70.00 M.I.B.; Skipper doll in "Learning To Ride" outfit #1935 (1965 booklet), $50.00 M.I.B.; Barbie doll in "Stormy Weather" outfit #0949 (1964 booklet), $25.00 M.I.B.; Skipper doll in "Rain or Shine" outfit #1916 (1964 booklet), $20.00 M.I.B.

Midge doll in "Knitting Pretty" outfit #0957 (1963 booklet), $35.00 M.I.B.; Skipper doll in "School Girl" outfit #1907 (1963 booklet), $25.00 M.I.B.; Barbie doll in "Aboard Ship" outfit #1631 (1964 booklet), $45.00 M.I.B.; Skipper doll in "Ship Ahoy" outfit #1918 (1964 booklet), $35.00 M.I.B.

Barbie doll in "Sporting Casuals" outfit #1671 (1965 booklet), $25.00 M.I.B.; Skipper doll in "Outdoor Casual" outfit #1915 (1965 booklet), $25.00 M.I.B.; Barbie doll in "Disc Date" outfit #1633 (1964 booklet), $30.00 M.I.B.; Skipper doll in "Platter Party" outfit #1914 (1964 booklet), $25.00 M.I.B.

Midge doll in "Fun 'N Games" outfit #1619 (1965 booklet), $55.00 M.I.B.; Skipper doll in "Sunny Pastels" outfit #1910 (1965 booklet), $25.00 M.I.B.

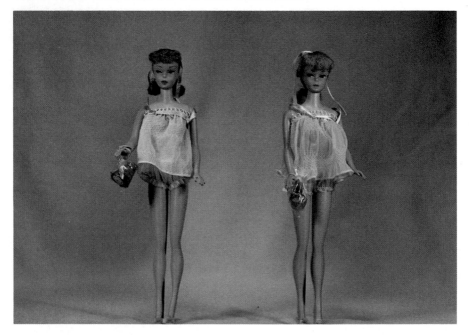

Barbie doll in "Sweet Dreams" outfit #973 (1961 booklet). This is not a hard to find outfit. What makes this unusual is the different color. "Sweet Dreams" came in yellow. Pink is a color variation and makes it hard to find. Pink only, $55.00 M.I.B.

Skipper doll in "Loungin' Lovelies" outfit #1930 (1965 booklet), $50.00 M.I.B.; Skipper doll in "Land And Sea" outfit #1917 (1964 booklet), $30.00 M.I.B.; Skipper doll in "Town Togs" outfit #1922 (1964 booklet), $35.00 M.I.B.; Skipper doll in "Chill Chaser" outfit #1926 (1965 booklet), $35.00 M.I.B.

Barbie doll in "Satin 'N Rose" outfit #1611 (1963 booklet), $40.00 M.I.B. This outfit did not come with a hat; it came with a pair of rose slacks. This outfit is known by two names – "On The Avenue" outfit #1644 (1964 booklet) and "Sunday Visit" outfit #1675 (1965 booklet), $60.00 M.I.B.

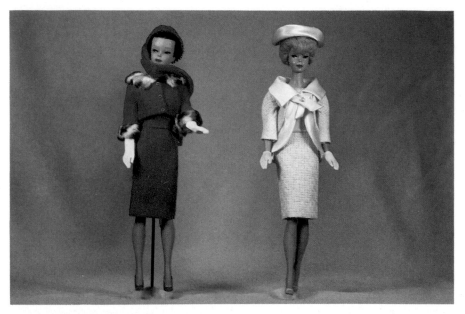

Barbie doll in "Matinee Fashion" outfit #1640 (1964 booklet), $70.00 M.I.B.; Barbie doll in "Fashion Luncheon" outfit #1656 (1965 booklet), $100.00 M.I.B.

,"Color Magic Fashion Fun" #4041 (1965 booklet), $60.00 M.I.B.; Barbie doll in "Stripes Away" outfit #1775 (1966 booklet), $55.00 M.I.B.; "Smart Switch" outfit #1776 (1966 booklet 3), $55.00 M.I.B.

Midge doll in "Skater's Waltz" outfit #1629 (1964 booklet), very hard to find, $70.00 M.I.B.; Barbie doll in "Print-A-Pleny" outfit #1686 (1966 booklet), $55.00 M.I.B.; Barbie doll in "Pink Sparkle" outfit #1440 (1966 booklet), $40.00 M.I.B.; Barbie doll in "Beau Time" outfit #1651 (1965 booklet), $25.00 M.I.B.

Barbie doll in "Sleeping Pretty" outfit #1636 (1964 booklet), $40.00 M.I.B.; Barbie doll in "Dreamland" outfit #1669 (1965 booklet), $25.00 M.I.B.

Ken doll in "Time To Turn In" outfit #1418 (pajamas) (1965 booklet), $35.00 M.I.B.; "TV's Good Tonight" outfit #1419 (robe) (1965 booklet), $35.00 M.I.B. This outfit is known by two names – "Slumber Party" #1642 (1964 booklet) and "Sleepytime Gal" #1674 (1965 booklet), $60.00 M.I.B.

Barbie doll in "Pink Moonbeams" outfit #1694 (1966 booklet), two color variations, $40.00 M.I.B.

Barbie doll in "Fashion Editor" outfit #1635 (1964 booklet), $45.00 M.I.B.; Barbie doll in "Saturday Matinee" outfit #1615 (1964 booklet), $75.00 M.I.B.

Barbie doll in "Invitation To Tea" outfit #1632 (1964 booklet), $60.00 M.I.B.; Barbie doll in "Country Club Dance" outfit #1627 (1964 booklet), $30.00 M.I.B.; Barbie doll in "Lunch On The Terrace" outfit #1649 (1965 booklet), $30.00 M.I.B.; Barbie doll in "Golden Evening" outfit #1610 (1963 booklet), $45.00 M.I.B.

Barbie doll in "Gold 'N Glamour" outfit #1647 (1964 booklet), $75.00 M.I.B.; Barbie doll in "Shimmering Magic" outfit #1664 (1965 booklet), $100.00 M.I.B.

Barbie doll in "White Magic" outfit #1607 (1963 booklet), $70.00 M.I.B.; Barbie doll in "Lunch On The Terrace" outfit #1649 (1965 booklet), $35.00 M.I.B.; Barbie doll in "Intrigue" outfit #1470 (1966 booklet), $65.00 M.I.B.

Barbie doll in "London Tour" outfit #1661 (1965 booklet), $65.00 M.I.B.; Barbie doll in "Poodle Parade" outfit #1643 (1964 booklet), $75.00 M.I.B.

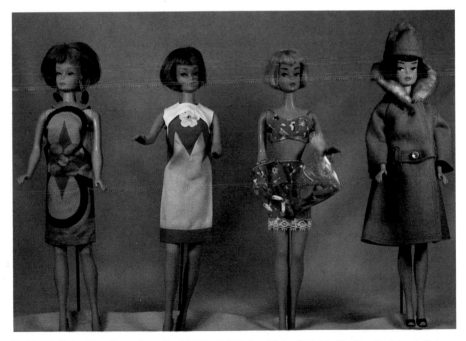

Barbie doll in "Sunflower" outfit #1663 (1966 booklet), $35.00 M.I.B.; Barbie doll in "Tropicana" outfit #1460 (1966 booklet), $35.00 M.I.B.; Barbie doll in "Underprints" outfit #1685 (1966 booklet), $30.00 M.I.B.; Barbie doll in "It's Cold Outside" outfit #0819 (1963 booklet), $35.00 M.I.B.

Barbie doll in "Beautiful Bride" outfit #1698 (1966 booklet), $150.00 M.I.B. This is the most beautiful wedding gown. It is very hard to find. Barbie doll in "Wedding Wonder" outfit #1849 (1966 booklet), $60.00 M.I.B.

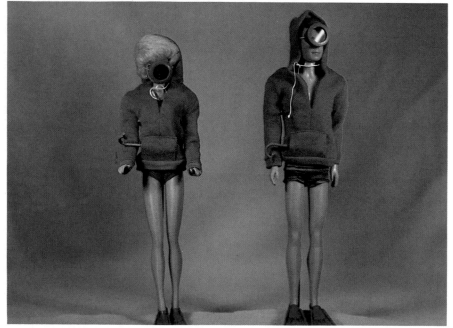

Barbie doll in "Barbie Skin Diver" outfit #1608 (1964 booklet), $25.00 M.I.B.; Allen doll in "Ken Skin Diver" outfit #1406 (1964 booklet), $25.00 M.I.B.

Barbie doll in "Music Center Matinee" outfit #1663 (1965 booklet), $75.00 M.I.B.; Barbie doll in "Pretty As A Picture" outfit #1652 (1965 booklet), $40.00 M.I.B.

Barbie doll in "Barbie Learns To Cook" outfit #1634 (1964 booklet), $75.00 M.I.B. Also called "Lunchtime" #1673 (1965 booklet); Midge doll in "Candy Striper Volunteer" outfit #0889 (1963 booklet), $55.00 M.I.B.; Barbie doll in "Junior Designer" outfit #1620 (1964 booklet), $50.00 M.I.B.; Barbie doll in "Knit Hit" outfit #1621 (1964 booklet), $50.00 M.I.B.

Barbie doll in "Travel Togethers" outfit #1668 (1966 booklet), $30.00 M.I.B.; Barbie doll in "Crisp 'N Cool" outfit #1604 (1964 booklet), $50.00 M.I.B.; Barbie doll in "Modern Art" outfit #1625 (1964 booklet), $60.00 M.I.B.; Barbie doll in "Black Magic" outfit #1609 (1964 booklet), $50.00 M.I.B.

Barbie doll in "Brunch Time" outfit #1628 (1964 booklet), $75.00 M.I.B. Also called "Coffee's On" #1670 (1965 booklet); Barbie doll in "Student Teacher" outfit #1662 (1964 booklet), $65.00 M.I.B.; Barbie doll in "International Fair" outfit #1653 (1965 booklet), $45.00 M.I.B.; Barbie doll in "Studio Tour" outfit #1690 (1966 booklet), $40.00 M.I.B.

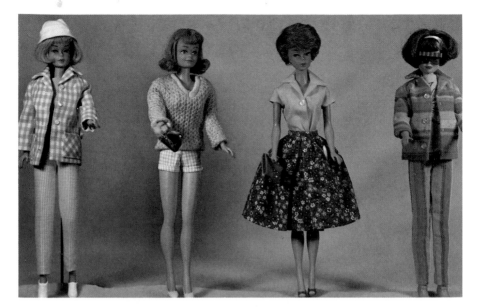

Barbie doll in "Outdoor Life" outfit #1637 (1964 booklet), $50.00 M.I.B.; Midge doll in "Vacation Time" outfit #1623 (1964 booklet), $35.00 M.I.B.; Barbie doll in "Country Fair" outfit #1603 (1963 booklet), $30.00 M.I.B.; Midge doll in "Trail Blazers" outfit #1846 (1966 booklet), $45.00 M.I.B.

Barbie doll in "Drum Majorette" outfit #0875 (1963 booklet), $40.00 M.I.B.; Midge doll in "Cheerleader" outfit #0876 (1963 booklet), $60.00 M.I.B.; Allen doll in "Drum Major" outfit #0775 (1963 booklet), $40.00 M.I.B.

Barbie doll in "Guenevere" outfit #0873 (1963 booklet), $60.00 M.I.B.; Ken doll in "King Arthur" outfit #0773 (1963 booklet), $70.00 M.I.B.; Barbie doll in "Poor and Rich Cinderella" outfit #6872 (1963 booklet), $70.00 M.I.B.; Ken doll in "The Prince" outfit #0772 (1963 booklet), $65.00 M.I.B.

Barbie doll in "Arabian Nights" outfit #0874 (1963 booklet), $65.00 M.I.B.; Ken doll in "Arabian Nights" outfit #0774 (1963 booklet), $75.00 M.I.B.; Barbie doll and Ken doll in "Red Riding Hood and the Wolf" outfit #0880 (1963 booklet), $125.00 M.I.B.

Barbie doll In "Barbie In Switzerland" outfit #0822 (1963 booklet), $65.00 M.I.B.; Allen doll in "Ken In Switzerland" outfit #0776 (1963 booklet), $65.00 M.I.B.; Barbie doll in "Barbie In Holland" outfit #0823 (1963 booklet), $55.00 M.I.B.; Ken doll in "Ken In Holland" outfit #0777 (1963 booklet), $50.00 M.I.B.

Barbie doll in "Barbie In Mexico" outfit #0823 (1963 booklet), $65.00 M.I.B.; Ken doll in "Ken In Mexico" outfit #0820 (1963 booklet), $65.00 M.I.B.; Barbie in "Barbie In Hawaii" outfit #1605 (1963 booklet), $55.00 M.I.B.; Ken doll in "Ken In Hawaii" outfit #1404 (1963 booklet), $55.00 M.I.B.

Barbie doll in "Barbie In Japan" outfit #0821 (1963 booklet), $125.00 M.I.B. This costume is the hardest to find of all the travel costumes.

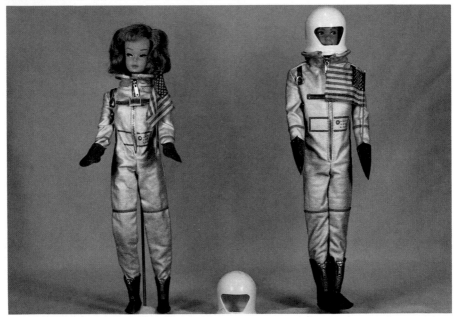

Barbie doll in "Miss Astronaut" outfit #1641 (1964 booklet), $175.00 M.I.B.; Allen doll in "Mr. Astronaut" outfit #1415 (1964 booklet), $175.00 M.I.B.

Skipper doll in "Masquerade Party" outfit #1903 (1963 booklet), $35.00 M.I.B.; Barbie doll in "Masquerade" outfit #0944 (1963 booklet), $35.00 M.I.B.; Ken doll in "Masquerade" outfit #0794 (1963 booklet), $30.00 M.I.B. These costumes are not hard to find singly, but are hard to collect in the complete group.

Steffie doll in "Kitty Kapers" outfit, one of the "Put-on's and Pets" sets. Very hard to find (1972 booklet), $125.00 M.I.B.; Barbie doll in "Fashion 'N Sounds Country Music" outfit (1971 booklet), $75.00 M.I.B.; Barbie doll in "Fashion 'N Sounds Groovin' Gauchos" outfit (1971 booklet), $75.00 M.I.B.

Steffie doll in "Party Lines" outfit #3490, $60.00 M.I.B.; Miss America "Majestic Blue" outfit, $90.00 M.I.B. Both of these outfits are "Miss America" outfits and are very hard to find.

Francie doll in "Quick Shift" outfit, Wards Exclusive (1965 catalog), $45.00 mint in package; Casey doll in "Style Setter" outfit, Wards Exclusive (1965 catalog), $50.00 mint in package; Francie doll in "Furry-Go-Round" outfit, Sears Exclusive (1967 Christmas catalog), $50.00 mint in package; Francie doll in "Prom Pinks" outfit, Sears Exclusive (1967 Christmas catalog), $55.00 mint in package. Although tagged, these outfits are hard to identify without the aid of a Sears or Wards catalog.

Barbie doll in "New Disco-Dater" outfit #1807 (not seen in any booklets), department store special from 1966, $50.00 mint in package; Barbie doll in "Glimmer Glamour" outfit (1968 Sears Exclusive), $75.00 mint in package; Barbie doll in "The Yellow Go" outfit (1967 Sears Exclusive), $60.00 mint in package.

Skipper doll in "Country Picnic" outfit #1933 (1965 booklet), $90.00 M.I.B.; Skooter doll in "Let's Play House" outfit #1932 (1965 booklet), $80.00 M.I.B.; Skooter doll in "Funtime" outfit #1920 (1964 booklet), $50.00 M.I.B.; Skipper doll in "Happy Birthday" outfit #1919 (1964 booklet), $65.00 M.I.B.

Skooter doll in "Sledding Fun" outfit #1936 (1965 booklet), $50.00 M.I.B.; Skipper doll in "Rainy Day Checkers" outfit #1928 (1965 booklet), $50.00 M.I.B.; Skipper doll in "Cookie Time" outfit #1912 (1964 booklet), $45.00 M.I.B.

Skipper doll in "Tea Party" outfit #1924 (1965 booklet), $50.00 M.I.B.; Skipper doll in "Can You Play?" outfit #1923 (1965 booklet), $30.00 M.I.B.; Skipper doll in "Dog Show" outfit #1929 (1965 booklet), $90.00 M.I.B.; Skipper doll in "Jeepers Creepers" outfit #1966 (1968 booklet), $25.00 M.I.B.

Ken Fashion Pak "Cheerful Chef" outfit, mint in package, $30.00; Ken doll in "Goin' Huntin'" #1409 (1963 booklet), $35.00 M.I.B.; Allen doll in "Fun On Ice" outfit #0791 (1963 booklet), $30.00 M.I.B.; Allen doll in "Roller Skate Date" outfit #1405 (1963 booklet), $30.00 M.I.B.

Barbie doll in "Floating Gardens" outfit #1696 (1966 booklet), $90.00 M.I.B.; Barbie doll in "Formal Occasion" outfit #1697 (1966 booklet), hard to find, $100.00 M.I.B.

Francie doll in "Clam Diggers" outfit #1258 (1965 booklet), $30.00 M.I.B.; Francie doll in "Concert In The Park" outfit #1256 (1965 booklet), $35.00 M.I.B.; Casey doll in "Gad-Abouts" outfit #1250 (1965 booklet), $30.00 M.I.B.; Casey doll in "Shoppin' Spree" outfit #1261 (1965 booklet), $40.00 M.I.B.

Francie doll in "Fresh As A Daisy" outfit #1254 (1965 booklet), $35.00 M.I.B.; Francie doll in "It's A Date" outfit #1251 (1965 booklet), $30.00 M.I.B.; Casey doll in "Tuckered Out" outfit #1253 (1965 booklet), $30.00 M.I.B.; Francie doll in "First Things First" outfit #1252 (1965 booklet), $25.00 M.I.B.

Black Francie doll in "First Formal" outfit #1260 (1965 booklet), $75.00 M.I.B.; Francie doll in "Dance Party" outfit #1257 (1965 booklet), $45.00 M.I.B.; Francie doll in "Polka Dots 'N Raindrops" outfit #1255 (1965 booklet), $35.00 M.I.B.; Francie doll in "Checkmates" outfit #1259 (1965 booklet), $35.00 M.I.B.

Francie doll in "Sweet 'N Swingin'" outfit #1283 (1966 booklet), $70.00 M.I.B.; on hanger, "Summer Frost" outfit #1276 (1966 booklet), $40.00 M.I.B.; Francie doll in "Two For The Ball" outfit #1232 (1966 booklet), $40.00 M.I.B.; Francie doll in "Waltz In Velvet" outfit #1768, $50.00 M.I.B., Francie doll in "The Lace Pace" outfit #1216 (1967 booklet), $45.00 M.I.B.

Francie doll in "Dreamy Wedding" outfit #1217 (1967 booklet), $60.00 M.I.B.; Francie doll in "Victorian Wedding" outfit #1233 (1966 booklet), $75.00 M.I.B.; No Bangs Francie doll in "Wedding Whirl" outfit #1244, $40.00 M.I.B.; Francie doll in "Bridal Beauty" outfit #3288 (hardest to find of the Francie doll wedding gowns), $45.00 M.I.B.

Ken doll in "American Airlines Captain" outfit #0779 (1964 booklet), $75.00 M.I.B. This set came with a duffel bag for one year only (1964). This bag is a bit larger and darker than the one in the Barbie doll set. Ken doll in "Army and Air Force" outfit #0797 (1963 booklet), $75.00 M.I.B.; Ken doll in "Sailor" outfit #0796 (1963 booklet), $35.00 M.I.B.

Ken doll in "Play Ball" outfit #0792 (1963 booklet), $45.00 M.I.B.; Ken doll in "Touch Down" outfit #0799 (1963 booklet), $45.00 M.I.B.; Allen doll in "Holiday" outfit #1414 (1964 booklet), $60.00 M.I.B.; Ken doll in "Campus Corduroys" outfit #1410 (1964 booklet), $50.00 M.I.B.

Ken doll in "College Student" outfit #1416 (1964 booklet), $70.00 M.I.B.; Allen doll in "Seein' The Sights" outfit #1421 (1965 booklet), $55.00 M.I.B.; Ken doll in "Country Clubbin'" outfit #1400 (1963 booklet), $50.00 M.I.B.; Ken doll in "The Yachtsman" outfit #0789 (1963 booklet), $75.00 M.I.B. This is the only time this set came with a hat.

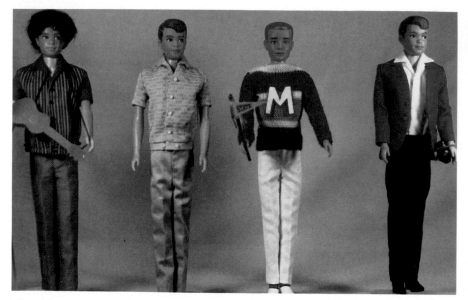

Allen doll in "Ken-A-Go-Go" outfit #1423 (1965 booklet), hard to find complete, $75.00 M.I.B.; Allen doll in "Jazz Concert" outfit #1420 (1965 booklet), $60.00 M.I.B.; Ken doll in "Campus Hero" outfit #0770 (1963 booklet), $35.00 M.I.B. This is the only year they used the letter "M" in place of the letter "U"; Allen doll in "Rovin' Reporter" outfit #1417 (1964 booklet), $40.00 M.I.B.

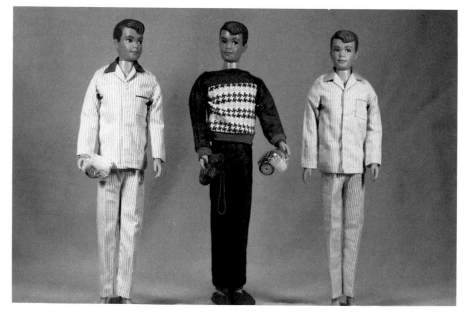

Allen doll in "Sleeper Set" outfit #0781 (1962 booklet), $20.00 M.I.B.; Allen doll in "Off To Bed" outfit #1413 (1964 booklet), $50.00 M.I.B.; Allen doll in "Sleeper Set" outfit #0781 (1963 booklet), $25.00 M.I.B. This is a variation in color and came out in blue for only one year.

Ken doll in "Summer Job" outfit #1422 (1965 booklet), very hard to find, $90.00 M.I.B.; Ken doll in "Business Appointment" outfit #1424, $200.00 M.I.B. This set did not come with the suit. Only the coat, hat and accessories were included. This is the rarest and the hardest to find of all the Ken outfits.

Dressed Box Dolls And Gift Sets

Skipper "Flower Girl" set #1904, $225.00 M.I.B.; Barbie "Icebreaker" set #942, $225.00 M.I.B.; Barbie "Barbie's Dream" set #947, $225.00 M.I.B.; Barbie "Career Girl" #954, $200.00 M.I.B.

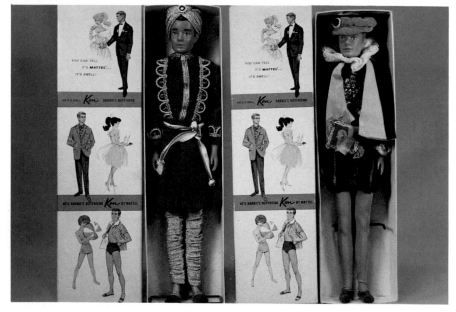

Ken "Ken Arabian Nights" set #074, $225.00 M.I.B.; Ken "The Prince" set, $225.00 M.I.B.

Barbie "Mix 'N Match Set" (1962), purchased at J.C. Penney, $400.00 M.I.B.

Barbie "Sparkling Pink Gift Set" #1011 (1963 booklet), $325.00 M.I.B.

Skipper "Party Time Gift Set" #1021 (1964 booklet), $225.00 M.I.B.

Skipper "On Wheels" gift set #1032 (1964 booklet), $250.00 M.I.B.

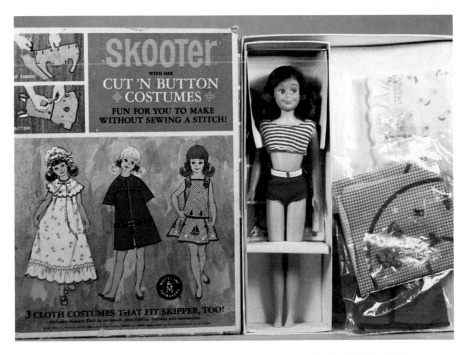

Skooter "Cut 'N Button Gift Set" (1967 Sears Christmas catalog), $200.00 M.I.B.

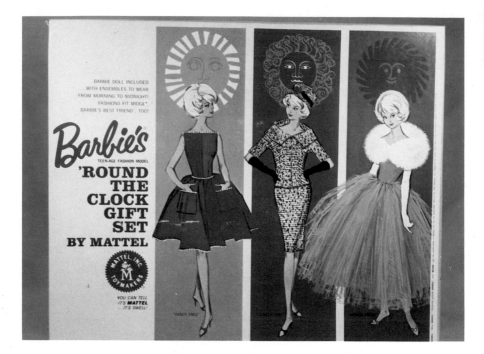

Barbie "Round The Clock Gift Set" #1013 (1964 booklet), $450.00 M.I.B.

Barbie "Wedding Party Gift Set" #1017 (1964 booklet), $550.00 M.I.B.

Barbie, Ken and Midge "On Parade Gift Set" #1014 (1964 booklet), $550.00 M.I.B.

"Francie and Her Swingin' Separates" #1042 (1966 Sears Special), $350.00 M.I.B.

Standard Barbie "Twinkle Town Set," $350.00 M.I.B.

Chris Gift Set (1967 Sears Christmas catalog), $250.00 M.I.B.

Talking Barbie "Pink Premiere" gift set #1596 (1969 booklet), $350.00 M.I.B.

Living Barbie "Action Accents" gift set #1585 (1970 Sears Christmas catalog), $350.00 M.I.B.

Francie "Rise 'N Shine" gift set #1194 (1971 booklet), Sears Special, $325.00 M.I.B.

Talking Barbie "Perfectly Plaid" set #1193 (1971 booklet), Sears Special. $325.00 M.I.B.

Malibu Ken "Surf's Up" set #1248 (1971), Sears Special, $250.00 M.I.B.

Walking Jamie "Strollin' In Style" gift set #1247 (1972), $350.00 M.I.B.

Skipper "Swing-A Rounder Gym" set #1179 (1972 booklet), $225.00 M.I.B.

Structures, Rooms And Furniture

"Barbie Fashion Shop" #817 (1962 booklet), $100.00 M.I.B.

"Barbie and Ken Little Theatre" #0490 (1963 booklet), $150.00 M.I.B.

"Barbie and Skipper's Schoolroom" (1965 Sears Christmas catalog), very rare, $225.00 M.I.B. (Thank you, Billy Boy.)

Small part of the furniture from "Barbie and Skipper's Schoolroom."

"Skipper Dream Room" #4094 (1964 booklet), $150.00 M.I.B.

"Barbie's New Restyled Dream House" #4092 (doll not included), $150.00 M.I.B.

"Barbie Goes To State College" #4093 (1964 booklet), $150.00 M.I.B.

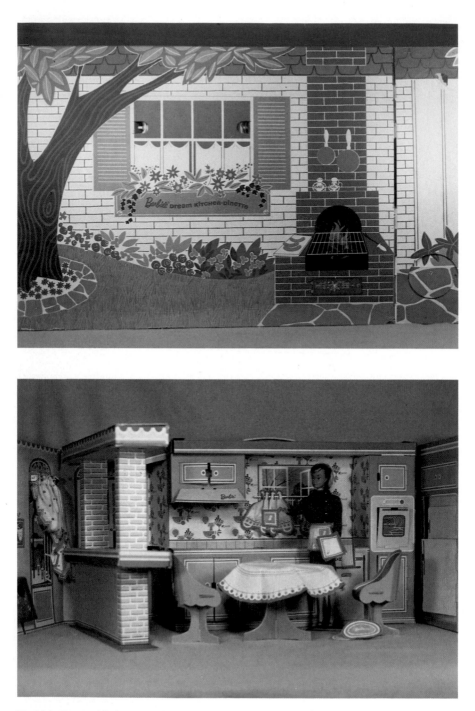

"Barbie's Dream Kitchen and Dinette" #4095 (1964 booklet), $150.00 M.I.B. This structure came with some most interesting accessories (doll not included).

"Tutti Playhouse" #3306 (1966 booklet). This playhouse came with a Tutti doll. $75.00 mint.

"Francie House" #3302 (1966 booklet). Doll not included, $25.00 mint.

"Francie and Casey Studio House" #1026 (doll not included), $25.00 mint.

"The World of Barbie House" #1048, $35.00 mint.

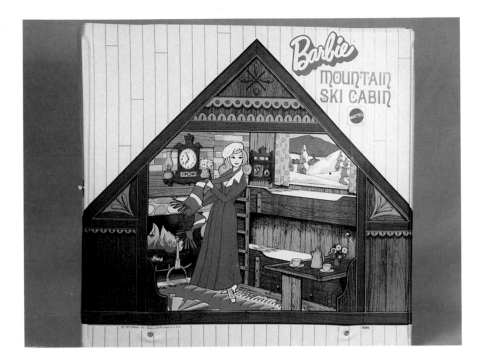

"Barbie's Mountain Ski Cabin" #4283, Sears Exclusive, $25.00 mint.

"Barbie's Country Living House" #8662, $35.00 mint.

"Barbie and Midge Queen Size Chifferobe" (Suzy Goose), hard to find, $75.00 mint.

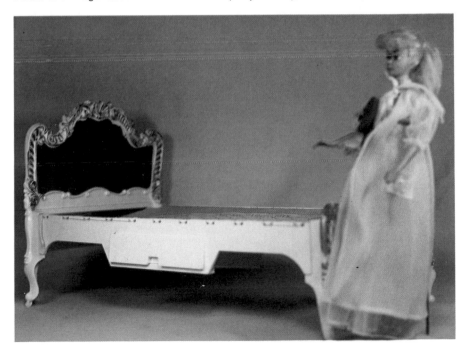

"Barbie Queen Size Bed" (Suzy Goose), very hard to find, $75.00 mint.

"Barbie's Four Poster Bed Outfit" (Suzy Goose), $20.00 mint; "Barbie Wardrobe" (Suzy Goose), $20.00 mint; "Barbie Vanity and Bench" (Suzy Goose). This came with a little throw rug, $20.00 mint.

"Ken Wardrobe" (Suzy Goose), $35.00 mint.

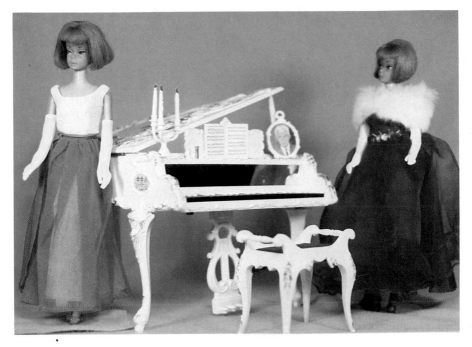

"Barbie's Music Box Piano and Bench" (Suzy Goose). Plays "I Love You Truly." This is one of the most sought after Barbie accessories, $200.00.

"Skipper Jeweled Wardrobe" (Suzy Goose), $35.00 mint; "Skipper Jeweled Bed" (Suzy Goose), $35.00 mint.

francie, Barbie's "Mod" cousin, has her own "Mod" A GO GO Bedroom Furniture

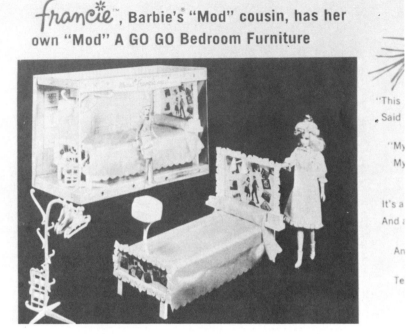

Tutti & Todd Go "DUTCH" with their exciting new bedroom furniture.

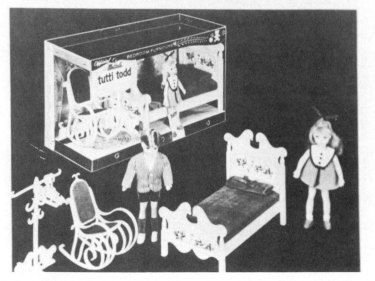

Francie "Mod A Go-Go Bedroom Furniture" set (Suzy Goose), very hard to find, $250.00 mint; Tutti and Todd "Dutch Bedroom Furniture" set (Suzy Goose), $250.00 mint. These photographs were taken from the November-December 1966 issue of Mattel's *Barbie Magazine.*

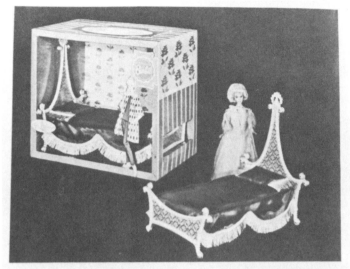

REGAL BED! Decorated with gold-like trim from head to foot. It's a bed fit for Sleeping Beauty with an elegant fringed spread and matching pillow of real taffeta. Isn't it dreamy?

"Barbie's Regal Bed" (Suzy Goose), $150.00 mint. Photo taken from the November-December 1965 issue of Mattel's *Barbie Magazine.*

"Barbie Lawn Swing and Planter" (Go Together Furniture), $100.00 M.I.B.

"Barbie Chaise Lounge" (Go Together Furniture), $50.00 M.I.B.

"Barbie Sofa-Bed and Coffee Table" (Go Together Furniture), $50.00 M.I.B. (Sofa cushions have been replaced.)

"Barbie Chair, Ottoman and End Table" (Go Together Furniture), $45.00 M.I.B. (Cushions have been replaced.)

"Skipper 'N Skooter Double Bunk Beds and Ladder" (Go Together Furniture), $65.00 M.I.B.

"Barbie and Skipper Living Room Furniture Group" (Go Together Furniture), $75.00 M.I.B.

"Barbie's Dining Room Furniture" (Go Together Furniture), $75.00 M.I.B.

"Barbie Cookin' Fun Kitchen," $35.00 M.I.B.

"Barbie Lively Livin' Room," $35.00 M.I.B.

"Barbie's Teen Dream Bedroom," $35.00 M.I.B.

"Barbie Room-Fulls Country Kitchen" #7404, $40.00 M.I.B.; Not shown – "Barbie's Apartment." It came complete with "Country Kitchen" and "Studio Bedroom" #9188. $60.00 M.I.B.

"Barbie Room-Fulls Studio Bedroom" #7405, $45.00 M.I.B.; "Barbie Room-Fulls Firelight Living Room" #7406, $45.00 M.I.B.

Toys And Accessories

Barbie Sports Car by Irwin Corporation, $100.00 M.I.B.

Barbie Hot Rod by Irwin Corporation, $150.00 M.I.B.

Close-up of different pony tail Barbie wristwatches.

Barbie Timepieces by Bradley. Top Row: "Barbie Starbright Boudoir Clock," $25.00 mint; "Barbie Fan Club Promotional Wristwatch," (1981) $40.00 mint. Bottom row: Early Barbie wristwatch with small dial, $50.00 M.I.B.; same watch with larger dial, $50.00 M.I.B.; pink watch with a variation in style, $50.00 M.I.B.; Barbie watch with ¾ face looking to the left, $50.00 M.I.B.; later Barbie wristwatch (1970's), $45.00 M.I.B.

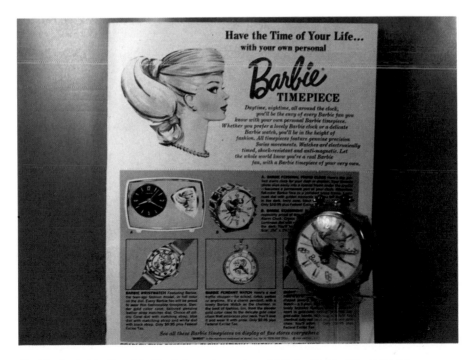

"Barbie Starbright Boudoir Clock," as shown in a Mattel's *Barbie Magazine* ad.

Barbie Electric Wristwatch Wall Clock, $40.00 mint. (Thank you Carolyn Mukrdechian and Judy Fryer.)

"Barbie and Francie Color Magic Fashion Set," $225.00 M.I.B.

"Dog 'N Duds" #1613 (1963 booklet), $140.00 M.I.B.

"Barbie Baby-Sits" #953 (1962 booklet), $150.00 M.I.B.; apron with color variation; "Barbie Baby-Sits" set (1964 booklet), $175.00 M.I.B. This set came without Barbie's accessories but has a baby layette added. Very hard to find complete.

Barbie's horse "Dancer," $55.00 M.I.B.

Barbie and Ken Dune Buggy by Irwin, very hard to find, $125.00 M.I.B.

"Barbie Fashion Stage" promotional ad.

"Barbie Fashion Stage," $30.00 M.I.B.

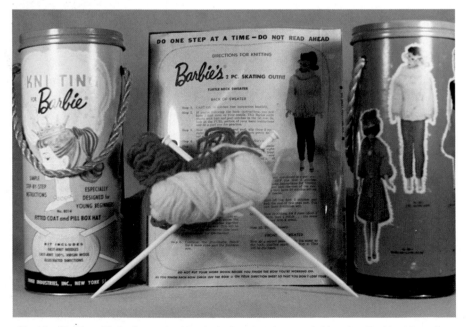

Top Row: Barbie lotion and original box and ad flyer (1961), $15.00 mint. Bottom Row: "Barbie Beauty Kit" (1961), complete, $20.00 mint. (Thank you Barbara Boury.)

"Barbie Knitting Kit," shown in March-April 1962 issue of Mattel's *Barbie Magazine.* $15.00 M.I.B.

"Barbie Heirloom Service" play set (1961), $50.00 M.I.B.

Barbie Record Tote (1961), $15.00 mint; Barbie Record Player by Vanity Fair (1961), $75.00 mint.

Top Row: Barbie Travel Case (1961), $15.00 mint; Barbie and Midge Travel Case (1963), $15.00 mint. Bottom Row: Barbie and Midge Lunch Box (1963), $20.00 mint; Barbie Thermos Bottle (1961), $15.00 mint; Barbie and Midge Thermos Bottle (1963), $10.00 mint; Barbie and Francie Lunch Box (1965), $10.00 mint.

Barbie Doll Case (1963), $10.00 mint; large Barbie Doll Case (1962), $10.00 mint; Barbie Doll Case (1961), $10.00 mint; Barbie Travel Case (1961), $15.00 mint.

Large Barbie Photo Album (1963), $25.00 mint; small Barbie Snap Shot Album (1963), $25.00 mint; Barbie Make-up Case (1963), $20.00 mint; Barbie Diary (1963), $25.00 mint.

Barbie Fan Club Bracelet, $15.00 mint; Barbie Play Ring, $50.00 mint in package; Barbie "Sweet 16" promotional necklace, $10.00 mint.

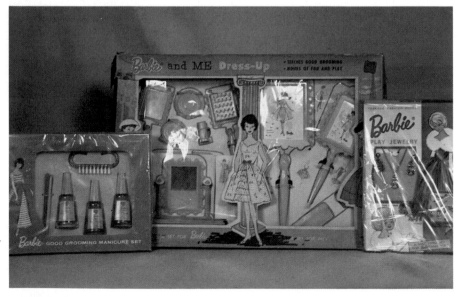

Barbie "Good Grooming Manicure Set," $25.00 mint; "Barbie and Me Dress-Up Set," $30.00 mint; "Barbie and Me Play Jewelry Set," $25.00 mint.

Very rare "Barbie Sings" demonstration record. This was never sold on the market, $75.00. "Barbie Sings" 45 rpm record album (1961), $25.00 mint.

Barbie "Mattel-a-Phone," $25.00 mint.

Unusual Cases

"Barbie Goes Travelin'" carrying case, $75.00 mint. Note each side is different. This case came in three colors — blue, pink, and yellow. Very hard to find.

Interior of "Barbie Goes Travelin'" case.

Barbie case with doll #2000 (1966 booklet). This case came with a Swirl pony tail Barbie doll dressed in a "Fashion Queen Barbie" suit. Very rare, $300.00 mint. (Thank you Paul Wrightsel.)

"Miss Barbie" carrying case by S.P.P., $35.00 mint; "Fashion Queen Barbie" carrying case by S.P.P, $30.00 mint.

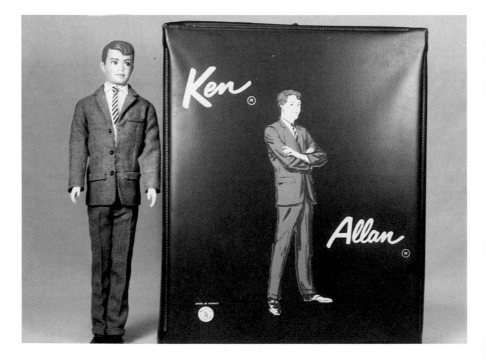

Ken and Allan case from France. Very hard to find, $75.00 mint. (Thank you Billy Boy.)

"Barbie Trousseau Trunk" with four compartments tor dolls, plus wig stand and hanging section. Very hard to find, $50.00 mint (doll not included).

"Barbie and Ken Costume Trunk" #5070 by S.P.P. (Standard Plastic Products, Inc.). Same interior as Trousseau Trunk, very hard to find, $60.00 mint.

"Tutti and Chris Patio Picnic" case, $25.00 mint.

Interior of "Tutti and Chris Patio Picnic" case.

Miscellaneous

"Barbie Sew-Free Fashion Fun," $20.00 each.

Counter-top display catalog, $75.00 mint. (Thank you Donna Lee Skonieczny.)

"The World of Barbie Fashions" store display, $600.00 mint.

"Barbie and Stacey Fashion Boutique" store display, $600.00 mint.

"The Wonderful World of Barbie" store display, $600.00 mint.

"Beauty Secrets Barbie" store display, $150.00 mint.

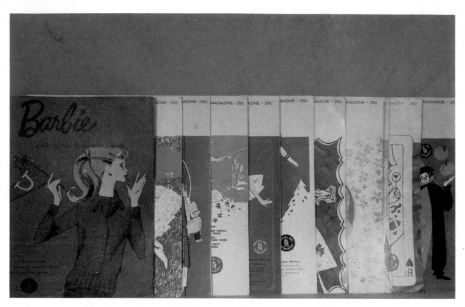

Assorted issues of Mattel's Barbie Magazine. $15.00 each.

Barbie Story Books by Random House. *The World of Barbie,* $15.00; *Barbie Cookbook* (not shown), very hard to find, $45.00 mint; all others, $8.00 each.